Free Verse Editions
Edited by Jon Thompson

M O 月 N

Chengru He 何珳茹

Parlor Press
Anderson, South Carolina
www.parlorpress.com

Parlor Press LLC, Anderson, South Carolina, 29621

© 2025 by Parlor Press
All rights reserved.
Printed in the United States of America
S A N: 2 5 4 - 8 8 7 9

Library of Congress Cataloging-in-Publication Data on File

978-1-64317-504-1 (paperback)
978-1-64317-505-8 (pdf)
978-1-64317-506-5 (ePub)

1 2 3 4 5

Cover art: "Full Moon and Autumn Flowers by the Stream" by Ogata Gekko.
c. 1895. Art Institute of Chicago. Gift of Mr. Allan Mitchell. Public Domain.
https://www.artic.edu/artworks/105935/full-moon-and-autumn-flowers-by-
the-stream
Book design by David Blakesley.

Parlor Press, LLC is an independent publisher of scholarly and trade titles in
print and multimedia formats. This book is available in paperback and ebook
formats from Parlor Press on the World Wide Web at https://www.parlorpress.
com or through online and brick-and-mortar bookstores. For submission
information or to find out about Parlor Press publications, write to Parlor
Press, 3015 Brackenberry Drive, Anderson, South Carolina, 29621, or email
editor@parlorpress.com.

Contents

Contents

For Jingyi Tan 談靜儀

MO月N

I The Moon

月

(a)

there is always a waxing crescent

                          between the new m**oo**n and her full phase
                rising   hanging herself
                               on top
                          of a pine

              a smiling eye
        looking West   blinking   measuring
                               time with her shadow

                    first   a curve
            another arm   softly reaching   cuddling
                  trees   deer   stars' secrets

        the ink slowly dries   cementing herself   on the inkstone
                               with the self from older times

              a black crescent
        on a new sheet of rice paper
                        in every tune
                               she utters

(b)

every month   the sea

    comes & goes   leaving
        a red m
          o o
          n

      on the tree
       of me

    somewhere birds
     are calling

the first fruit under the branch
            unripe

           unborn

  (never ask

    where it goes)

(c)

rising

        from the top left

                a swollen
                   belly

          from a belly
a m **oo** n   to be born

                  rising
                  (as the stroke bends
                      toward the earth)

(d)

when you learn 日 you learn 月

sun & m**oo**n
together   they bring light   明
& tomorrow

never ask
the open-ended 月
what kind of light
does she invite

to her
b **o** dy

(e)

as I am typing
y – u – e

snow comes from the sky
in silence

the lost part
of me
sneaks back
to remind the rest

of me
how I used to
hold a pen tight
one stroke
after another   the third   the fourth

or in another life
how my hands
tattooed

by ink stains
that burn
into

the black m **oo** n

(f)

from branch
    to branch
the m **oo** n follows

    eyes
      tired
of 0s and 1s
    flickering
    on a 13-inch screen

even though
it can reproduce a million m **oo** ns
in a millisecond
same shape   size   color

(where is my smiling crescent?)

(g)

one can write a book about one character, 月, m **oo** n

the modern version of 月 comes from its oracle ancestor, the shape of a waxing crescent. our ancestors were looking at the same m**oo**n, copied its shape on the tortoise shell. a small curve, a big curve. everyone who writes has written down 月 has written about 月. Li Bai's m**oo**n still shines upon the bed the window the ground

one can recite a hundred lines that 月 lives in. they are different they are the same m**oo**n

one, two, three, four. a small curve, a big curve, a short line, another. how we make m**oo**ns on paper

the many m**oo**ns live inside a b**o**dy. 脖, neck, 肚, belly, 肘, elbow, 臂, arm, 腕, wrist, 腿, leg, 脚, foot, 肤, skin, 脑, brain, 肝, liver, 肺, lung, 肾, kidney, 脊, spine . . . in every part of a b**o**dy lives a m**oo**n

one, two, three, four. a small curve, a big curve, a short line, another. how we make m**oo**ns and their friends on paper. grind the inkstone, flatten the paper, dip the brush, count four strokes, make m**oo**ns, before we learn how to type *y-u-e* on a computer to make a digital m**oo**n

a *yue* rises on the screen, becomes 月

a *yue* rises, grows full, summons the tide. blue tide from the ocean, red tide from a female b**o**dy. once a month red tide comes and goes. 月经, moon-flow. in my body lives a red m**oo**n

how many red m**oo**ns are there upon the sea

a 月 rises, under its costume, 11100110 10011100 10001000. it's the same moon it's different than the m**oo**n I made on paper for the first time

for tonight's party, which costume is she going to wear

II Postcards to Jingyi • Moonlight Variations

New Year

since when yesterday
has crossed the border you are
in the new year I am
in the old between us
thirteen hours
        of stars and m**oo**n

        to copy your dish
use thumb to press
down the gluten balls use chopsticks
to stuff the filling until
the hand feels the weight my hands
smell like lard use utility
bills to fill the mailbox today
        repeats yesterday

        to rinse
my hands under the water
for thirty seconds to apply
pass in front of *time* to recite
bian cha zhu yu shao yi ren
        missing a hand

        old sound
of an old poem the weakest
star marks the end
of the old sky today
becomes yesterday
        tomorrow

Moonlight Variations [Li Bai's Moon I]

chuang qian ming yue guang

yi si di shang shuang

ju tou wang ming yue

di tou si gu shiang

床前明月光
疑是地上霜
舉頭望明月
低頭思故鄉

Sunflower

Dear *en-na*   thinking of you
how was the moon of mid-autumn
did you share a mooncake
with someone from the past
here the sun is bright
I walk from block to block taking
pictures[1] of every wild
sunflower put *forever*[2] for their expiration date[3]
I walk in strange neighborhoods passing[4]
unknown blossoms and gnomes[5] the untended
fruits[6] on the ground the wet soil[7]
from sprinklers[8] it leads me back
home after a few turns[9] a loop[10]
back to the lush green on the porch[11]
the desk and the open notebook waiting[12]
for the next line[13]

------

1. Jingyi walked from home
2. all the way to Shiliu-Pu Marina holding
3. the baby in one arm
4. carrying
5. a big yellow fish in another
6. to find her husband
7. the early morning drizzles
8. of Shanghai 1951
9. the huge dock
10. a young mother and an infant
11. the sun was bright
12. the moon
13. had disappeared

Moonlight Variations [Li Bai's Moon II]

bright moonlight in front of the bed
looks like the frost on the ground
look up   the bright moon
look down   think about hometown

The Last Emperor

once or twice, you took me
to see an old factory-friend
or a *yipo*, distant
cousin of yours. it was
a sunny day, or it was
raining. we'd take one bus
then another, walk
into strange alleys, cough
out smoke from coal
-cake stoves. once,
not twice, you took me
to the cinema. it was
a matinee of *The Last
Emperor*. or a night. full
moon. I was the same age
as little Puyi, who still had
a wet nanny at four. the dark
theatre was full
of grown-up heads. I sank
into the giant womb. years later
you'd say *I've been
to the cinema*, and wait
for me to fill in the rest,
how, for example, Puyi's third
bride blows a white
feather, how, the wall
of light blinded me, pulled
me in, to fly
with the feather, how, later,
you took my hand, *we need
to go*, I dragged
my legs. we watched
five more minutes at the back
of the theatre. the movie
is long, Puyi grows old.
pulled me again, your hand, faint
smell of flour. we might

have had *cainue wenden*
at noon. hidden
moon. you might have sliced
the left-over wrappers, boiled them
with water, eaten as plain
noodle, while filling my bowl
with *wenden*, fat as pigs.

Moonlight Variations [Li Bai's Moon III]

moonlight falls
upon the bed
is like
frost
on the ground

I look up
the bright moon
looks back

I lower
my head
think
of
gu shiang

Leaf

start a day sweeping the leaves
fallen overnight. the broom joins
early birds, prepares a space for daily
practices. *cua, cua, cua...* on my

morning path the leaves are piled, one heap
after another, along the gridded streets, guarding
the sunlight. somewhere a leaf blower is herding
the brown bodies, before the rain

muddies the trail. why do we never ask a leaf
how far it wants to travel, if it wants to stay
with the storm, rupture, become the dust?

Moonlight Variations [to take out the moon I]

to take the m **o**   **o**   n
                    out
                        from the sky
to take the m   **o**
                            o   n

                    out
                    for a walk
leaving   the fr **o** st   on the gr **o** und
                    two sparr **o** ws
                    in
                        the nest b **o** x
            red
        cl **o** vers
            in O ct **o** ber

Time

on the day of *lidong* – the start
of winter – we turn the clock
back an hour leaves keep falling
regardless of human time[1]

someone in a wheelchair
stopped me[2] *is it the third or the fourth*
a question[3] I don't ask when[4]
the answer is in my pocket[5]

some answers[6] will never come:
when my message arrives[7]
on your screen are you finishing[8]
up morning exercise chatting[9]

with neighbors walking upstairs or lounging
on the sofa listening[10] to the *tick-tock* wondering
how soon[11] will the spring wind revisit[12]

you are fifteen hours ahead[13]

---

1. at nineteen Jingyi left the village
2. to big Shanghai. it was
3. a Wednesday or a Thursday. drizzles
4. on her hair
5. she does not know
6. some trips
7. have no return, only revisit
8. in dreams when the moon
9. is bright, lighting
10. her bed
11. how the flowers in her dreams
12. never wither
13. is mystery

Moonlight Variations [to take out the moon II]

                              to take the   m   **o**   **o**   n   out
                                                        of the line

                                                       & replace it
                        with an L E D 3 c **o** l **o** r t e
                            m p e r a t u r e l a m p

                                      to see your h   **o**
                                                  m   e
                                                  t   **o**
                                                  w   n

                                             on a 4K screen

                                          review the p **o** em
                                              with stars

Cat

remember the orange tabby in your old house? who knocked
on your door at five in the morning, came as he pleased but never

stayed. back then none of us knew about *chongwu*, pet, about ownership
of another life, about naming. we'd call every cat *maomi*, watching them

strolling in and out freely, napping in the sun. soon a *maomi* became two,
gave birth to small *maomi.* The little paws grew big in no time, disappeared

unannounced on a random day. soon the first subway line started running,
the old house was removed, you widowed. we have one blurred

picture of the old house with the cat. I have forgotten our last hug,
as I stroll foreign streets, searching. it's been

too long that I haven't knocked on your door. I walk around and greet
whomever I encounter along the way. a cat and her autumn.

Moonlight Variations [to take out the moon III]

to take the 月 out
          from its mother tongue

             & replace it
        with an alien sound

          & c
          u
             r v e s
        on the blank page

to make the m-o-o-o-o-o-n sound
        & repeat

        & repeat
        & put a star beside it

Humidity

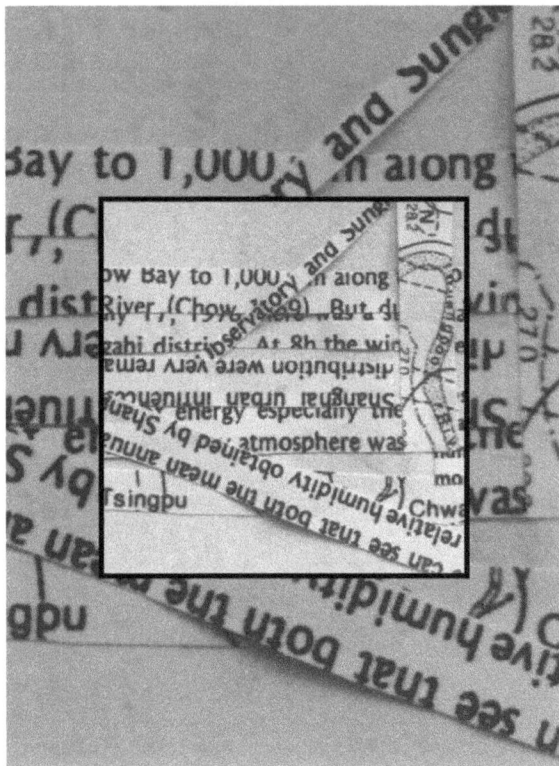

the place I moved to   is dry I miss   the humidity   in
Shanghai we used to   measure humidity   by how long
it took   the clothes to dry   bring the duvet   out on
a bamboo pole once   the sun was out   count   the
brown   dots on book pages knowing   were the gift   of
huangmeitian /yellow-plum-seasons   in transit to the cold
days   the leaves let go   the water in their bodies their
way   of slowly saying goodbye I use   a thermometer to
control   moisture   inside its various forms window con-
densation dews   on morning leaves sweat   from dreams
reading scales   in Fahrenheit translating them   back   to
the memories of skin on the calendar   tonight   the waxing
gibbous moon is bringing   tide

Moonlight Variations [to look for home I]

to look down

                    & stare into the space

           between your feet

          m **o** ss   r **o** cks leaf

         苔   石   葉

               that turns

            another verse

                to dust

            report only

           the shape

             between your feet

Green

how're the peonies on your balcony? sunlit
on the sixth floor, they're used to construction
noise and radio waves. you'd prune stems
above the buds, paint blossoms on *xuan* paper
with thick red, by pavilions and hills
you've never seen. *chun feng you lu*
jiang nan an – spring wind again greens
the southern bank, silently, leading your brush
with its hand. to turn a color into motion,
Wang Anshi casts our mind in a green direction
—*green* greens the blooming, our attention
on the page. the red sprouts take their time
to catch the eleventh century sun.
in your palm, the slowness of green.

Moonlight Variations [to look for home II]

to make t w o   c i r c l e s with your hands & to put them
                              on your e y e s

                              report only

                              the silver
                                      thing you see & call it
                                              h

                                          o

                                          m

                                          e

Park

someone invented the name, keeping bird chirps, leaves, footprints from memories, tied it to childhood like a balloon.

木 plus 木 is 林, one tree plus another becomes a wood.

on Sunday a green plastic coin slid into the ticket box, opened the park gate for my timid feet. turn right, monkeys' home. turn left, magnolia in bloom.

after you were widowed you started going to the park for the choir. the park was renamed after Lu Xun, whose mustache appears in every Chinese textbook.

a city and its park, parading in blues.

someone will show us the routes behind the trees and rocks, draw lines and circles, signs of pleasure and danger.

a seed graduates from a park, brings oars to see different seas.

in Liberty Park the birds from the North lounge on thin ice, shedding foreign squeaks. in the US parks have no gates.

木 plus 林 is 森. a wood invites more trees and becomes the forest.

a park and its trees, guarding the wind.

the man feeding the birds is all in black. he pronounces the *r* in *Iran*, where he comes from, without rolling his tongue.

Moonlight Variations [to look for home III]

to move a *roof* and a *pig*
    from one land to another
    & place them
    by the thick, large trees

to move a 宀 and a 豕
    from Shanghai to Salt Lake City
    & place them
    in zipcode 84102

to remove the tags
    from the luggage
    & place t-h-e
    in front of the nouns

to recite Jing Ye Si in mind
    chuang qian ming yue guang
    & replace the m**oo**n
    in the luggage
            & the language

宀 plus 豕 is 家
    a *roof* plus a *pig* is h**o**me

Gravity

now – *gravity* – a word
we quietly live in
how we name the coming of rain
      – rain – drop –
on a familiar hand   the weight[1]
of moisture   memories a feather[2] argues
with the wind

here in Salt Lake City[3] every step
is a ripe fruit from the high branch reminding[4]
my feet *you are going somewhere*
the crunch[5] of dry leaves records my
steps accumulates[6] the distance
from home *when are you coming back*[7]
I try to explain *travel ban*[8] to you

soon the moon will grow full
again returning[9] high waves to the bank
the grasshopper will jump
and fall[10]on its next leaf matching its color[11]
with the wrinkles of time
in dreams I cup my hands[12] to feel
a drop of rain from the past

---

1. Jingyi lifted
2. the heavy handle on the machine her face
3. turning red in the non-stop factory line
4. she didn't have time
5. to rest or think
6. about her two young children
7. *when are you coming back mama*
8. she didn't know she wouldn't know
9. until the next full moon
10. if the night was dark
11. and a pair of hands
12. lit a candle

Moonlight Variations [to invite the subject]

the moonlight in front of the bed
is like the frost on the ground
(he/she/they) look up   the bright moon
(he/she/they) look down   thinking of (his/her/their)
hometown

how to invite the non-self   from its nonexistence   to a
land of identity politics   how to introduce the non-self
who controls the verbs with no rules   to endless
pronouns   how to assign it a Social Security number   a
permanent address   & a color   choices one has to make
when submitting   herself/himself/themselves   to the
unknown

Flour

after Yehuda Amichai

outside your old home
there was a communal yard
outside the yard
a telephone booth
beside the booth
a flour shop
I wish I could go back
three more times

watch the flour
slide down from the silver tube
into a cloth bag
the air blooming white

I wish I could join the childhood me
& kick a rooster-feather *jianzi* high
& forget about your warning
don't go beyond the flour shop

I wish the indigo grandpa
would wait for me
in his duck-tongue hat
his shoes leaving prints
on the white-dusted ground

it was long
before the old
neighborhoods were
knocked down
or the day I took
a three-hour bus ride for a glance
of a crush's face
in the spring
drizzle

I wish I could slide
down like the flour
into a cloth-bag
pass the telephone booth
this time I wouldn't be scared
of that big black dog

Moonlight Variations [to reinvent the subject]

the moonlight
             in front of the bed
       is like
the frost
          on
       the ground
          look up   the moon
          look down   thinking
          of hometown

who is looking up
             in the line
     a cat   a tree
       or the moon
                      herself
       who looks
             up and sees
             her

                     r

                        e

                           f

                 l

                    e

                 c

              t

                      io

                 n

the missing subject
          at large   for over a century

           replace it
with anybody
          with any b o d y
who has the license
             to control the wheel
                 & the desire
             to control the verbs

order a coffee
        to go   your relationship
            with   the letters
        on the paper cup   exists
            while the liquid
                        lasts

The Sun

I want to tell you about the sun, but where should I start?

trying to describe something you see every day. *I've had more salt than the rice you've had,* you'd say. something

rises day after day in the same direction, in nursery rhymes and songs, in the eyes that look for the light. never complains

about the world it sees. something bright, hot, glowing, but that could also be tender, red, caressing a brown leaf on the vine before it leaves.

is there anything new I can tell you

about the world I see, the time I spend between new lands, new faces, old objects refreshed by new terms?

or it doesn't matter if I repeat myself, after the same greetings, saying aloud *taiyang* again, or *tayang* – closer to your native tongue. that my voice hasn't changed

is all you care about. that I hear you, we touch through hearing. that between us the fifty-four years, the sun rises

and falls, resets the color of a gloomy night. generous

with its time, especially in the last lines.

II Postcards in Jueju / 絕句

1

spring   river   flower   moon   night

night   flower   moon   river   spring

river   moon   night   spring   flower

post   code   like   feed   share [imperative]

2

like the FB (re)posts the snow keeps falling

the snow keeps falling into Liu Zongyuan's *cold-river*

the fisherman disappears from the poem

— snow, solitude, their future phase — *ciao*!

3

there was no future phase or tense for the white coming

from the past or enjambment on Mr. Liu's lonely

locust-boat. like one's beard, the lines insist on their shape,

direction, limit. *a volta? are you out of your mind?*

4

balance and couplets received odes, but a *turn*

is an orange in the cherry orchard, shivering. punctuations

were aliens, too. how. water. flows. back. and. forth.

as time loosens its sense = ~~past/present/future~~ = timelessness

5

a deer from Tang dynasty has lived is living will be living

a line is alive is dead was dead after the Enter key

she who is red will become has become me is me

[who] is the subject in this line

6

[whose] spring is late for the night cruise?

[whose] moon is drunk and forgets about the light?

[I] drink the spring the night the moon

my moon my time my embarrassed relationship with [I]

7

the speaker decides to put on the peacock

-feather hat & make an appearance at twelve

— *what a specific time!* — imagine the speaker's voice,

palms, eyes, the way she walks to fetch the moon in the river

8

me: what's that golden-yellow thing, broken in the water?

the speaker: Li Bai's loyal drinking buddy — oh, you like the feather?

the feather (羽): my image-based cousin, 月, where's your son?

the moon: I am satisfied with the double fullness in my body; don't question.

9

now, a blossom should happen with the full moon

the moon and the petals elope to your mind

the poet is *fishing the snow alone*

you and I are both strangers to the river

10

the one who retreats from the line offers

you, my reader, a full jar of bubblegum, naturally-flavored-pun

even the thinnest crescent has her full phase coming

even in this little four-line jar

IV Variations in Past Tense

Father Came Home, 1964

this morning the coal cakes, softened
by the night rain, used up five matches.
It rained so much this winter
in Shanghai. the cold grew with the mold.
I lit the sixth when he came
by the porch. this middle-aged man
looked at me. I him. we were
about the same height. neither of us
said anything. simply looking
at each other. he might be smiling,
but I was not sure. somehow I knew:
it's him. he went inside,
dropped a faded indigo bag
by the chair, took off the heavy
sheep fur-lined coat – the kind I'd only seen
a few times in pictures: in the North people wear
for the coldest nights – hung it
on the back of the chair, sat down, did not reach
for his bag. I forgot where I laid
my eyes, possibly the collar
of the fur coat. I hadn't seen him in years.
never, I meant. they said I have his lips.
I knew he's somewhere, not knowing
exactly where. I knew he's gone
for some reason, not sure
about exactly why. I poured a glass
of boiled water from the blue thermos flask.
the wooden cork dropped, bounced
to the iron stove – once burned
every photo and his past – I picked up
the cork before I handed him the glass.
Still hot. he took it over with both hands.
Thank you. the steaming glass stayed calm
in his dry callused hands, holding
no longer pens. he glanced
at my army green schoolbag, as if it were
a common day before the new year, I was just
off class, and he off work, *what did you learn
in Maths?* the same time I muttered
I need to get back to the stove.

Andante ma non Tanto

for dinner she compares
a lime dress with a jade one
three times

love
forgives its absurdity, the captioned simplicity
of limbs and lips, occasionally, if lucky, frees itself
from a good luck knot, the nothingness

of all

[melodic music]

the tangle of words, however awkward, keeps sending your run-on
tongue

to my shore
I'm busy searching for seashells
and short lines
once you found a perfect spot

perhaps in Japan

[drumbeats]

online profile says *I'm both Arthur and Lancelot*
she knows how to swipe

right, ranks a tray
of less frequently used words

[acoustic guitar ballad]

duh duh duh on Basho's door
green lingers   too much contrast
for an idealized winter

the frog has gone for a hike

[melodic music]

she senses his tempo
without weighing boots
and risk, deftly dissembles
a syllable, breaks its echo, plays
hair in strict meters, learns
to relieve the stress

behave
leave
before the meter maid is back
exemption
from the unredeemed promise

she likes the escape-room
he doesn't mind escape, but maybe a room first

respect natural order

[upbeat rock music]

a samurai has enough patience
until the snow comes   the code of eyes unfreezes the myth of cold
three months of snow
in its metamorphosis

departure
is not always fun
some call it a walk, downward dog, herbal tea
take all the walnuts from the bread, I'll have the cranberries
leftover, the pond, a potential
splash, the collective

silence

to which we both contribute
anonymously

[sound of nature]

the game of hint and link
has a long history   she attempts to interpret a four-leg table

into a quatrain   he frowns
how about fishing? hiking? fishing and hiking? something
outdoors   up there there's a good pond

she appreciates a metaphoric downpour

[sound of nature, drumbeats]

with trained ears no break is needed
five-seven-five
recite my name in one breath   I'm there

and you cannot come
up here. measure love in a different language, report the pattern.
the last cicada is hanging for a future metaphor.

a samurai knows how to cut

a line, kaiken sheathed
tight

[mysterious string music]

stillness stirs

the distance between them   she measures the complexity
of air, wonders if there's a good place for unused and useless ~~words~~, unzips

a meaningful look

[bells]

can Basho be Basho without the fire? tame a line before it gets tired. the
residue

of long verses

58

speaks of your eyes

what is left unrhymed is synchronized with heartbeats

practiced in foggy mornings
we can hear each other but cannot
touch

[sound of typewriter, sound of strings, sound of nature]

a sheet of whispers

when he's about to come she says *let's talk
about the wage gap*

[sudden silence]

Andante ma non Tanto

      faster! but not too much

[delicate music]

Andante ma non Tanto

      faster! but not too much

[fading sounds]

Visiting a Friend on a Snowy Night

Tonight the moon is quiet. Fresh
white covers the world. Fallen

branches all over. I want to row
a boat like Wang Huizhi, to your

door, before the next snow, to see
your light. One foot plus another

is two feet – my feet recognize only
the Milky Way in your mind, a silver

railroad crossing snow
-covered land. I walk and walk, as if

smelling the petals in your
teacup. The cold eats my ears.

Behind me the miniature city blocks
flicker. Quiet in quietness, no echoes

from the sky. The Jin Dynasty snow
keeps falling. You stay in poetry

with Dai Kui, light him a cigarette;
he pours you the snow-brewed tea,

in silence, both expecting an unpromised
knock. Wang Huizhi's night boat

is waiting. The creek is covered in snow.
I walk and walk, like Wang, no longer

care where I'm going. Passion's hand
melts snow, cools down in the white.

By your door, a late cicada. In my pocket,
a pair of horse chestnuts from the fall,

now dry and hard, clank in time
with my homebound feet.

Mountain Life on an Autumn Evening

—Letter to Wang Wei

Dear Wang Wei, thinking of you
      as I hike into the untamed
            nature in Montana, western
                 land in *mei guo*, far away

from your *white-water-bright*
白   *-field.* Here, my feet meet rocks
水   and creek, greet butterflies,
明   frogs, striders, while gravity
田

keep toes heavy. Here, I pick red
      berries, make an *mmmmm* sound as they explode
            on my tongue. Here, I run
                into you, *the clear water flows*

over stones, pine trees erect
      against the rocky
          walls. Your lines come
             alive, though no washerwomen

明月松間照
清泉石上流

return from the bamboo groves.
      The mountains are not strange. You are waiting
          for me. I don't need to tell you more
             about hummingbirds – tiny

helicopters hovering
      around nectar, ground squirrels' labyrinth
          of burrows, or in the morning, how
             black cows' mooing travels

along the endless blue ridges, their echoes
      mooing back. I'm sure you know
          all the shades and sounds well as you know
            your moon and trees. 平 平 仄 仄 平
                     Ping ping ze ze ping

up, down, flat. The bees are making
    hives in your lines. The spider arrests
        a fly that attacks your rhyme
            scheme. . . 仄 平 仄. You didn't
              Ze ping ze

drive hours, drop by the gas station in Idaho
    that hangs *lottery* and *bathroom* signs
        in Chinese, pass dozens of *stop* and *slow down,*
            before you finally sit in a cabin

in the national bird refuge, and write words
    that perhaps will please a few
        friendly ears. Or maybe
            you did, and we never asked – how

many pairs of self-sewn shoes were worn
    out before you found that perfect pine
        and line? Your blistered heels, stained
            ink brushes, the loneliness

you drank that never made its way
    into your poetry. The bamboo grew quietly
        by your hut. On rainy days the leaves
            broadcasted sorrow.

I guess you're not interested in the nineteen
    ways of looking at you and your deer, or arguments
        on the colors of mosses, as 青 is not
            only blue or green, it is also the measure

of time, the opposite of the gray
    hair at your temples. But I know you'd feel at home
        with the grass and clouds here, and by night,
            the slowly rising stars would cast

away the blue poetic feet. 平 平 仄 仄 仄 平 平
Ping ping ze ze ze ping ping

Dear Wang Wei, if you read the letter, come

for dinner. I'll share my potatoes and look

for your autumn moon among the pines.

Persimmons

It's almost winter, two weeks before Christmas, leaves
turn brown overnight, covering the quiet pavement. Most people

are gone. Home and fire. I can hardly remember
what autumn looks like. There they are.

Two persimmons, one bigger, one smaller, leaning
against each other, in the darkening winter light, on their way

of shrinking and withering, centered on your vintage side table.
There's nothing else, only the persimmons.

What are they for? You're not supposed to eat persimmons
at this stage. Either fresh or sun-dried is fine. These two reddish

fruits, gravitated by time, cured by silent gazes, challenge
reviewers. How I fail to explain what they are.

In China persimmons are different. They come in ancient scrolls,
come with chrysanthemums and crabs, come as memories, puckery

and sweet. You buy them when they're hard, eat them when they turn
soft. In between many days of wonder. Poke one from time to time

to catch the best timing. When it's ready your finger would tell.
It's the fruit of patience, of waiting. It took me years

to learn how to eat a persimmon. But I simply say
Li-Young Lee writes about them. These two quiet creatures,

too bright in the dusk, inviting themselves into a new poem
of old words. You are currently reading.

Four Kinds of Emptiness

of which one is full, awaiting
a virgin blossom

to unbalance the abundance.
the room is quiet, as if we are

part of the plan,
planted, pressed, bound, blessed.

the empty receives attention.
a leaf flutters, *please,*

more light. in the shade
of fear, Queen Anne's Lace speaks,

in time the roots will grow.
the empty is accurately placed,

carefully touched
by its shadow.

we happen to agree
on going back to the first day

of imagination, where each leaf
is light, and empty is full.

Notes

"Humidity": the text in the image is from Chow, Shu Djen, and Chao Chang. "Shanghai Urban Influences on Humidity and Precipitation Distribution." *GeoJournal*, vol. 8, no. 3, Springer, 1984, pp.

"New Year": the last line of 王维Wang Wei's poem "Thinking of my brother on Double Ninth", one of the most well-known classic Chinese poems on traveling and missing home. The whole poem goes like "alone on the alien land/ (I) miss my home most on festive days/ my brothers climb high with dogwoods / planting them everywhere only / missing a hand".

"Mountain Life on an Autumn Evening - Letter to Wang Wei" uses the same title as Wang Wei's "Mountain Life on an Autumn Evening" (王維 "山居秋暝").

"Four Kinds of Emptiness" responds to Lorrie Lane's oil painting.

Acknowledgments

To my poetry mentors and friends Katharine Coles and Craig Dworkin, I am beyond grateful for our conversations that sparked part of the book. I would also like to thank Joel Brouwer, Robin Behn, Hank Lazer, Jacqueline Osherow, Paisley Rekdal, and Heidi Staples.

I am grateful to all my friends who have read the earlier drafts of some of these poems. Special thanks to Jasmine Khaliq and Jamie Smith.

Poems from this collection have appeared or are forthcoming in the following journals: *Colorado Review, Gulf Coast, Kenyon Review, Poet Lore, Poetry Northwest, Tint Journal, and Watershed Review.* I would like to thank the editors of these journals. My thanks to the AWP Intro Journals Project.

I would also like to thank the Taft-Nicholson Center, the Creative Writing program at the University of Alabama, and the Creative Writing program at the University of Utah.

Thanks to my family.

Thank you, *en-na*, for reading Tang poems to my ears before I developed memories.

About the Author

Chengru He 何琤茹 is a poet and translator from Shanghai. She is the author of a hybrid collection *I Would Vanish into Its Stronger Existence* (Wet Cement), the Chinese translator of two books and a few chapbook projects. Her writing, translation, and multimedia works appear in *Ancient Exchange, Colorado Review, Fence, Gulf Coast,* and *The Kenyon Review,* among others. A former EFL teacher, she is currently based in Salt Lake City, where she is a PhD candidate in English Literature and Creative Writing at the University of Utah.

Photograph of the author by Joel Brouwer.
Used by permission

Free Verse Editions

Edited by Jon Thompson

www.ingramcontent.com/pod-product-compliance
Lightning Source LLC
LaVergne TN
LVHW091231080426
835509LV00009B/1236